ESCAPING AN ANIMAL ATTACK

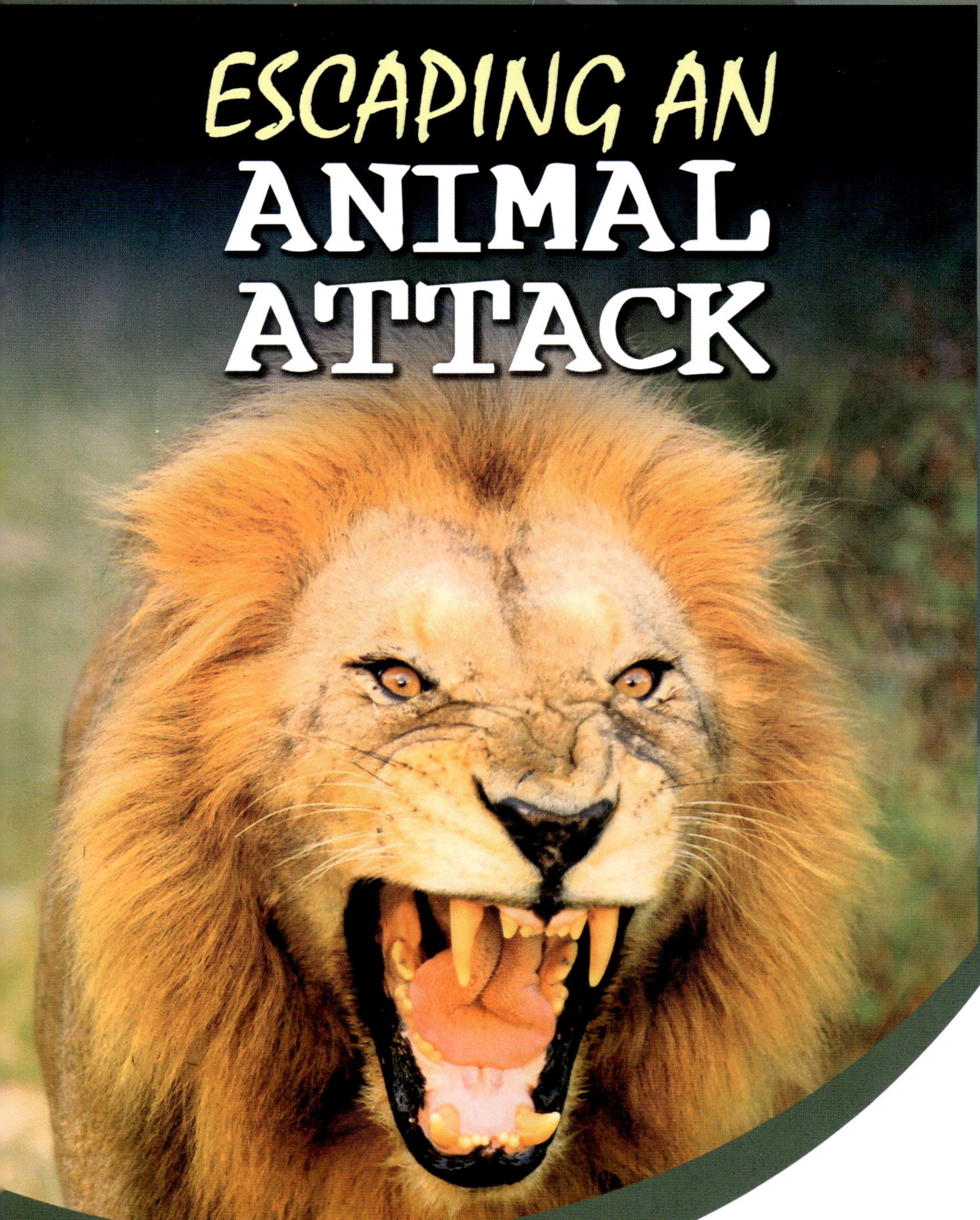

BY ALISHA GABRIEL

The Child's World®
childsworld.com

Published by The Child's World®
1980 Lookout Drive • Mankato, MN 56003-1705
800-599-READ • www.childsworld.com

Photographs ©: Dave Pusey/Shutterstock Images, cover, 1; Mark Higgins/Shutterstock Images, 5; Ramon Carretero/Shutterstock Images, 6; Wonderful Nature/Shutterstock Images, 8; Sergey Uryadnikov/Shutterstock Images, 9; Evident Images/Shutterstock Images, 10; Shutterstock Images, 12, 14, 21; Avner Ofer Photography/Shutterstock Images, 17; Enrique Aguirre/Shutterstock Images, 18; Thomas Eisenhuth/picture-alliance/dpa/AP Images, 22; Joe Burbank/MCT/Newscom, 23; Jack Nevitt/Shutterstock Images, 24; Chase Dekker/Shutterstock Images, 27

ISBN 9781503825260
LCCN 2017959689

Printed in the United States of America
PA02377

TABLE OF CONTENTS

FAST FACTS

- Animal attacks are rare. Most wild animals avoid people.
- In the ocean, great white sharks hunt seals. When a seal swims to the surface to breathe, the shark swims up and attacks. In the shadowy water below, a person on a surfboard looks a lot like a seal. Many shark attacks on people are probably cases of mistaken identity. From 1837 to January 2017, there were 1,344 shark attacks on people in the United States.
- More than one million alligators live in Florida, but attacks on people are uncommon. From 1948 to 2016, alligators attacked 388 people in the state. In almost 70 years, only 24 people in Florida have died as a result of an alligator attack.
- From 1990 to September 2004, lions attacked people more than 800 times. Some lions attack people because they cannot find wild prey.

It's important to not approach wild animals. ▶ If you do come close to a wild animal outdoors, remember to always stay calm.

- Experts estimate that 1,500 grizzly bears and more than 300,000 black bears live in the United States. Between the years 2000 and 2017, 27 people died from bear attacks in the United States. Experts recommend that hikers make lots of noise, stay alert, and carry bear spray, a peppery-smelling spray that bears don't like. If hikers see bears, they should stay at least 100 yards (91 m) away.

Chapter 1

GRAPPLING WITH A GREAT WHITE

On August 26, 1998, 16-year-old Jonathan Kathrein picked up his best friend Sean and drove to Stinson Beach in Northern California. It was the last day of summer before their junior year of high school. In the parking lot, Sean pulled their blue surfboards from the back of the car while Jonathan picked up his water bottle, sweatshirt, and blue gym bag.

Sean grabbed his yellow and blue towel, Jonathan slid his keys in his pocket, and they walked toward the ocean. They put their things on an empty spot on the beach and ran into the water. Other surfers dotted the water, but there was plenty of room in the **vast** ocean.

They swam until they were 50 yards (46 m) from the shore. The water was only 6 feet (2 m) deep, but there were enough waves to surf there.

◄ **Experts estimate that when sharks attack humans, they are just taking a "sample bite" to see if humans are food or not.**

Someone spotted a dark fin above the surface of the water and shouted, "Shark!" Jonathan, Sean, and the other surfers swam as fast as they could toward the beach.

A huge, sleek body jumped out of the water. A few seconds later another one followed. Dolphins! It was a false alarm.

▲ **Some surfers wear wetsuits to keep warm in the cool water. To a shark, this could look like a seal or other animal underwater.**

▲ **It may seem like shark attacks are common due to stories in the news, but they are actually very rare.**

Jonathan and Sean stayed in the water to catch more waves. The ocean water was very cold, though. When they heard the shrill sound of the noon whistle, Sean said, "I'm heading in to the beach to warm up."

"Okay, I'll catch one more wave and ride it in to join you," said Jonathan.

Jonathan floated on his surfboard and waited for the next wave. Suddenly, he felt cold. And alone. The waves had carried him away from the other surfers. He paddled and kicked to line himself up with the lifeguard station on the beach, but as he pulled his hand through the water, it bumped something solid and rough. He looked around but couldn't see anything in the shadowy water. He sensed something was in the water near him.

▲ **Beaches are typically closed after a shark attack to make sure it is safe before people return to the water.**

Jonathan paddled fast and kicked toward the beach. Moments later, a great white shark smashed into Jonathan and knocked him off his surfboard. Jonathan was dragged underwater. The shark's teeth cut like razors into his right leg, and pain shot through his body. The shark pulled him away from the shore and violently shook him.

Jonathan realized the shark was trying to rip off his leg. His lungs burned, and he knew he needed to breathe air soon.

He tried to wrap his arms around the shark, but it was too big. He couldn't reach its eyes. Then he spotted the shark's gills. He slid his fingers into the shark's gills and held on.

The shark let go of Jonathan's leg, and he swam to the surface to breathe. He didn't know if the shark was still there, or why it let go. It was a second chance, and he took it. He swung himself onto his surfboard, his bleeding leg hanging in the water, and paddled with his arms.

As he got closer to shore, Jonathan called for help. People turned to look at him but didn't understand what was happening. No one came to help him. He had to save himself. He used the rest of his energy to reach the shore.

Jonathan stopped in the shallow water of the beach and lay his head on his board. A teenager ran toward him and pulled Jonathan out of the water. People shouted, "Shark! Shark!"

Others raced to help Jonathan. Swimmers rushed out of the water. Twenty minutes later, a helicopter took him to the John Muir Health Center in Walnut Creek, California, for surgery. Doctors worked on his leg for eight hours, putting in hundreds of stitches and staples to save it.

At the end of the next week, Jonathan went home from the hospital. A large banner stretched across the front of his house announcing, "Home of the World Famous Shark Wrestler!"

Chapter 2

IN THE LION'S DEN

In February 2015, 15-year-old Neha Sharma and her parents flew from Sydney, Australia, to South Africa on vacation. Neha loved animals and had dreamed of going to Africa for years. She couldn't wait to see animals in the wild. She and her parents traveled to Kudus Rus Game Lodge. It was located approximately two hours from Johannesburg, South Africa.

Mr. Loots, a ranger at the lodge, took the Sharmas on a tour. They saw many animals and met lion cubs, too. Neha sat on the ground under a tree with three cubs. One tan cub lay on the ground facing Neha. She petted its head and took pictures on her phone. Two other cubs played nearby, pawing and biting each other.

When they left the cubs, Mr. Loots wanted to show the family more animals. The family walked for a while, following Mr. Loots, not sure where they were going.

◄ **To lions everything that is made of meat, including humans, is food.**

▲ **Game lodges are large areas of land where wild animals can live safely.**

Neha's parents fell behind, but Neha kept up with Mr. Loots. He stopped outside a large enclosure, opened the gate, and walked in. Five two-year-old lions paced inside the cage. Mr. Loots approached a lioness and petted her head.

He asked Neha if she wanted to pet it. At first, she shook her head no. But Mr. Loots told her the lion was used to people, so Neha stepped into the cage.

Neha looked into the lion's eyes, but something didn't feel right. She changed her mind about petting the lion and turned to leave the cage. Out of the corner of her eye, she saw a tan blur in the air.

The 300-hundred-pound (136 kg) lioness attacked Neha and knocked her to the ground. Neha felt the lion bite her arms and chest. Then the lion moved up. The lion's sharp teeth bit into her head. She fainted from the pain.

A male lion attacked Mr. Loots, and the other three lions circled them. The lions were blocking the entrance to the cage. Neha's parents screamed and ran toward the cage. Her mother quickly ran inside, but then the other three lions charged at her.

WHEN LIONS ATTACK

Lions are stealthy predators. Without claws or horns, humans might seem like defenseless prey to a powerful, hungry lion. In the case of a lion attack, people should not turn their backs to the lion or run away. Lions can run 50 miles per hour (80 kph). Safari guides tell people to wave their arms above their heads, yell, spray the lion with pepper spray, and throw things at the lion. If the lion stops moving, try backing away slowly. If it moves again, freeze!

Neha's father pulled his wife out of the cage and closed the lions inside.

Panicked, Neha's father screamed and called out for Mr. Loots to help Neha. A lion bit Mr. Loots's neck, and he stopped moving. Neha's father thought Mr. Loots had died. He knew it was up to him to save his daughter, or die trying.

But suddenly Neha woke up and started hitting the lion. Her punches were so powerful that she bruised her own arms. She pushed to her feet, ran out of the cage, and swung the metal gate closed behind her.

Neha looked down at herself, covered in her own sticky, red blood, and realized what had happened. Her legs felt weak, and she fell down again. Her father ran to her, picked her up, and carried her all the way back to the lodge.

At the hospital, Neha needed surgery for her **injuries**. The lion had attacked her head, neck, chest, thighs, and arms. Mr. Loots had survived and was treated for minor injuries.

Looking back, Neha doesn't blame the lion. She believes wild animals should live in the wild, not in a cage. Neha fought back and Mr. Loots "played dead," but both were lucky to survive a lion attack.

Female lions typically do all of the hunting for their pride in the wild. ▶

Chapter 3

AN ALLIGATOR ATTACKS

On August 7, 2014, in St. Cloud, Florida, nine-year-old James Barney Jr. rode his bike near Lake Tohopekaliga with a friend. It was a hot Thursday afternoon.

There were signs posted that said not to swim in the lake. But James hopped off his bike and jumped in while his friend waited on the pier.

Suddenly, James felt something brush up against him in the water. He thought someone was playing with him. But when he reached down into the water, James felt the rough jaws and sharp teeth of an alligator. The nine-foot (2.7 m), 500-hundred-pound (227 kg) alligator opened its massive jaws. It bit down on James hard. The alligator's teeth gripped James's right leg, backside, and **abdomen**.

◄ **Alligators can blend in with water to hide from their prey. Sometimes they just look like a floating log.**

A DANGEROUS SURPRISE

Alligators are patient predators, hoping for a surprise attack. When people encounter alligators on land, they can usually outrun the reptiles, who aren't interested in a chase. The real danger is an attack in water. Once an alligator locks its jaws on prey, it will go into a "death roll," either drowning its prey, or letting it bleed to death. Experts advise swimmers to splash, scream, and fight back if an alligator attacks. Poking a finger into the alligator's eyes might cause enough pain that it will open its jaws.

James fought back. He hit the alligator over and over again until he felt it loosen its grip. Then he reached inside the predator's mouth and tried to force it open.

The alligator loosened its grip on James. But the alligator's sharp teeth scratched James's skin as he slipped free. James yelled for help as he swam to shore, and people ran over to pull him out of the water.

James's friend called 911. An ambulance quickly arrived, followed by a helicopter. Emergency workers rushed to help James into the helicopter.

Alligators can go six months to a year without eating. ▶

▲ **If a sign is posted near a body of water that says "No Swimming," be sure to pay attention.**

Then James was airlifted to the Arnold Palmer Hospital for Children in Orlando, Florida.

Once James arrived at the hospital, he was **examined** by the medical staff. One of the staff members pulled a large alligator tooth out of James's skin.

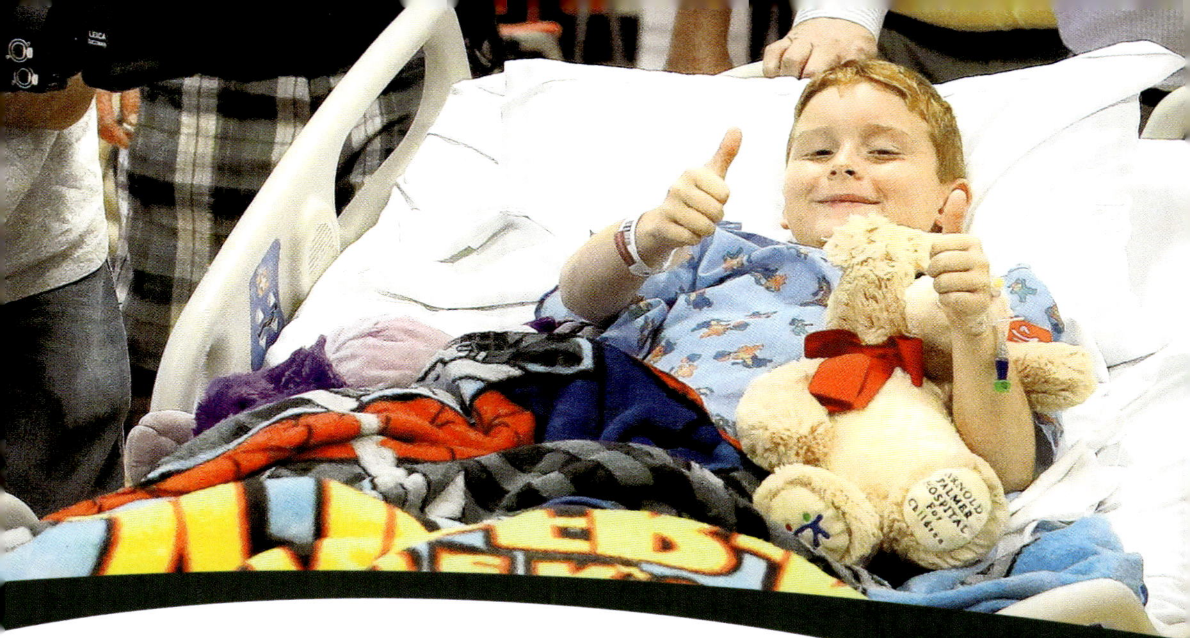

▲ **James smiling from his hospital bed in 2014**

Members of the Florida Fish and Wildlife Conservation Commission (FWC) took the tooth to help them identify the alligator that had attacked James. Trappers were already out looking for the alligator.

Reporters flocked to the hospital to meet James and get an update on his condition. James's father sat near him as he rested, propped up in a wide hospital bed. James held a tan teddy bear with a red ribbon around its neck.

Dr. Ross Morgan, who treated James when he arrived, told reporters that James did not need surgery. James had approximately 30 bite marks and scratches on his skin. But he would be okay. James learned a lesson that day. He knew he would never swim in that lake again.

Chapter 4

BATTLING THE BEAR

Jim Cole began studying animals in the wild in 1991. He took a special interest in grizzly bears. On May 23, 2007, Jim went hiking in Yellowstone National Park in an area of Wyoming called Hayden Valley. The melting snow dripped from some sagebrush, filling the air with its fresh scent. Jim walked several miles without seeing any bears.

Jim decided to take a break and headed back toward his van. As he walked down a small hill, a mother grizzly suddenly came out of nowhere. Her baby cub was nearby. The mother bear was only 10 feet (3 m) away from Jim. She charged at him. The bear tackled Jim to the ground, pinning his right arm under his body. He was unable to reach his bear spray. The bear clawed at his face and head. Jim felt his head crunch under her weight. He stayed still until the mother and her cub ran away.

◂ **Grizzly bears are typically active only at night and during dawn and dusk.**

Jim stood up. He didn't know how bad his injuries were. But he knew he needed medical help as soon as possible. The walk back to his van would be too hard. He decided to walk toward Trout Creek, where tourists often stopped to look at the scenery.

Jim could barely see because of his injuries. He used the hazy sun as a guide to walk in the correct direction. As he stumbled along, he wondered, "How could this be happening to me again?" Almost 14 years earlier, Jim had accidentally surprised a grizzly bear in Glacier National Park in Montana. The bear scratched a 4-inch (10 cm) gash on the back of Jim's head and broke his wrist. Jim didn't blame the bear. It had acted in self-defense, and this second attack was similar. The mother bear was protecting her cub.

Jim kept walking and focused on finding help. He tried not to think about his injuries. He walked for at least a mile before he heard rushing water. He figured he was close to Trout Creek and about one mile (1.6 km) from the road. Jim needed to find help soon.

Judy and John Taylor were tourists at Trout Creek. They pulled out their binoculars and looked around Hayden Valley. Then Judy saw Jim limping by the side of the creek. They saw two coyotes circling behind him. Judy and John realized he needed help.

▲ **Mother bears are fiercely protective of their young cubs. They will attack anything they think is a threat.**

John went down to get Jim and carried him closer to the road. Strangers stopped to cover him with jackets and blankets. Then they waited for an ambulance. The skin of Jim's face hung down. Four claw marks stretched from his neck up to his forehead. He didn't seem to have eyes, a nose, or a mouth anymore, but somehow Jim was still breathing.

MOST LIKELY ANIMAL ATTACKS

As of 2017, these are the number of people killed per year by the animals below.

Mosquito	725,000
Snake	50,000
Dog	25,000
Snail	10,000
Crocodile	1,000
Hippopotamus	500
Elephant	100
Lion	100
Wolf	10
Shark	10

An ambulance and a helicopter transported Jim to the Eastern Idaho Regional Medical Center Emergency Room. Dr. Dan Hinckley, an ear, nose, and throat **surgeon**, performed surgery on Jim to **reconstruct** his face. It took more than 1,000 stitches and staples to put Jim's face back together.

Although Jim lost sight in his left eye and needed many more surgeries, he didn't give up on living. On September 1, 2007, Jim hiked back to the scene of the attack. A month later, he drove to the hospital in Idaho to thank the doctors and nurses who saved his life. He started exercising, wrote a song about the bear attack, and wrote a book. It is called *Blindsided: Surviving a Grizzly Attack and Still Loving the Great Bear.* Jim plans to spend many more years studying grizzlies.

THINK ABOUT IT

- In your opinion, should animals that attack humans be hunted and killed, or should they be allowed to live? Please explain your answer.
- If someone is hurt in a state or national park, should the government pay their medical bills? Why?
- Jonathan Kathrein returned to the water a few years after his shark attack, and Jim Cole returned to the scene of his bear attack. What benefit do you think victims of an attack hope to gain from returning to the scene?

GLOSSARY

abdomen (AB-do-men): The abdomen is the section of the body below the chest and above the hips, also called the belly or stomach. The alligator that attacked James bit into his abdomen.

examined (eg-ZAM-end): When something is examined, it is looked at very carefully. When James arrived at the hospital, Dr. Ross Morgan examined his injuries, looking carefully at the bites and scratches to decide what kind of treatment James needed.

injuries (IN-juh-reez): Injuries are damages or harm. After the lion attacked Neha, she needed surgeries for her injuries.

reconstruct (ree-kuhn-STRUHKT): To reconstruct something means to rebuild it or re-create it. Dr. Hinckley operated on Jim to reconstruct his face after a bear attacked him and damaged his head and face.

surgeon (SUR-jin): A surgeon is a type of medical specialist who can perform surgery on people who are sick or injured. The ear, nose, and throat surgeon saved Jim's life after the bear attack.

vast (VAST): Vast means huge in size. Before Jonathan was attacked by the shark, he sat on his surfboard and looked at the vast ocean.

TO LEARN MORE

Books

Dubowski, Cathy East. *Shark Attack!* New York, NY: DK Publishing, 2015.

Tarshis, Lauren. *Nature Attacks!* New York, NY: Scholastic Press, 2015.

Ventura, Marne. *How to Survive an Animal Attack.* Mankato, MN: The Child's World, 2016.

Web Sites

Visit our Web site for links about escaping an animal attack:
childsworld.com/links

Note to Parents, Teachers, and Librarians: We routinely verify our Web links to make sure they are safe and active sites. So encourage your readers to check them out!

SELECTED BIBLIOGRAPHY

"Boy Recounts Gator Attack in Press Conference." *Today.* NBC Universal, 9 Aug. 2014. Web. 3 Nov. 2017.

Cole, Jim, and Tim Vandehey. *Blindsided: Surviving a Grizzly Attack and Still Loving the Great Bear.* New York, NY: St. Martin's Press, 2010. Print.

Eveleth, Rose. "How to Survive a Lion Attack." *Smithsonian.* Smithsonian Institution, 3 July 2013. Web. 3 Nov. 2017.

INDEX

ABOUT THE AUTHOR

Alisha Gabriel lives near Austin, Texas, and has been teaching for 20 years. She writes about people, music, history, and nature. This is her third book for children.